MW01224460

SO YOU WANT TO BE A PSYCHIC

By

ROBIN ROBERTS

Copyright © 2015

FORWARD

We are all born with a sixth sense. As Yoda would say the force is strong within each of us. Some strengthen this sense with practice, some are simply born with a more developed psychic antenna and some close their ears to the Angels, Guides and the Creator. But no matter which one you are there will be something within these pages for you.

TABLE OF CONTENTS

SO YOU WANT TO BE A PSYCHIC?

So you want to be a psychic? You have watched every episode of the Medium and are sure you can do what she does because really how hard can it be? I don't want to shatter any illusions but the life of a psychic is not as exciting as it is made out to be. A lot of what you read or see is media made up hype.

Its true for some of you the gift of insight will flow effortlessly, words will spill like a fountain of knowledge from your mouth. But do you really 'know' what being a psychic will entail?

When you read for someone they become a passenger and you are the one taking them on a journey and whether they reach their destination safely is all in your hands. Some Psychics are very flippant about the information they give out. As long as they are getting paid they don't really contemplate the words which come forth. This may come as a surprise to most but you are not meant to open your mouth and let what's in your head out on every occasion.

That is what we call 'psychic gossip' which is no

different than overhearing a conversation which wasn't meant for you but repeating it anyway. This is why we have a little thing called 'asking permission'. This is when we respect the persons right to choose whether they wish the information or not.

It isn't only about 'reading' people and 'seeing the future'. The people who come to you are people who have feelings, emotions and are vulnerable just like you. It isn't a game like so many think when they first start tuning in and increasing their intuition.

It isn't about doing party tricks, it isn't about people thinking you are a great psychic it, isn't about you at all its about the person sitting opposite you. And if it is about you then you are in the wrong business.

Here's another news flash. The words Psychics utter are very powerful, only because people have this belief Psychics are somehow all knowing. Bottom line is it's the people you read who give the words power, they just haven't figured it out yet. But this raises the question of whether information should be filtered or shared in a different format than it was given. It also begs the question - what is in the person's highest good.

So you see, being a Psychic is not all cut and dry, and knowing the how and when is something which only comes with experience. I may know your husband is having an affair, but really is it in your highest good to know this?

This information is not only going to change your life but your children's and even your spouses as well. Would I be better to ask for guidance for you which will help you become a stronger, more self assured person, one who will cope if things fall apart? Maybe fate is better left in the hands of a Creator who knows what he/she is doing.

You not only have to know what to do with the information you get but also the information being requested.

"I want to know is he the one" The one-line answer may be - no he is not but ponder this - sometimes people enter our lives with lessons which we need to learn in order to grow as spiritual beings. So you give out a simple "no he is not" she dumps him based on your 'advice' and moves onto the next relationship and two months later she is back asking the same question.

Why? Because it wasn't about him at all it was about her inability to form healthy relationships. So what would have happened had you said "here are the roadblocks which are stopping you from forming healthy relationships" or "you need to build a healthy sense of self and here are a few ways to do this."

Yes, it takes a little bit longer than the standard 'yes/no' replies but this is someone's life you are talking about and being an intuitive is not a party trick or a neat game to amuse yourself with. I have picked up the pieces many a time and helped people put their lives back together all because someone with a little

Psychic ability thought they were the next John Edwards.

People think that if they learn the symbols of tarot and angel cards this automatically makes them psychic. When in fact, all it makes you is someone who can read the instructions which come with the cards. It isn't that simple. There are a lot of other factors which come into play.

You may walk away feeling good about yourself because you have shared all this wonderful information but remember this, every word you utter will create a seed of thought. And these thoughts can be very powerful if someone believes without question in them.

So before you pick up a packet of tarot cards or start sharing your new found abilities or throwing words around in reckless abandonment find someone who can guide you through the process. Get some experience and learn the ropes so to speak.

These are people's lives you are dealing with and as such everything should be done with honour, dignity and respect.

I cannot repeat often enough the fact you are dealing with vulnerable people and their lives. Being a psychic is not something to be taken lightly as words can have great power and if you haven't had the learning to go with the gift, you could do a great deal of damage very easily.

The lessons to follow are designed to not only increase your intuitiveness but to get you thinking about things like ethics, empathy, and the ways in which the gift of insight can be used. It is not designed to turn you into a fortune teller. My goal is to turn you into someone who empowers people by helping them create their own futures, by giving clarity and understanding.

But most of all they are designed to help you become more in tune with your own life....

Myth: Psychics can read minds

Fact: Psychics cannot read minds they cannot go into your head but they can step into your energy and this is what they read.

What are the different types of psychic ability?

Clairsentience: *This is the ability to get information from impressions received. People with this ability are sometimes called empaths because they are able to "feel" the emotions of others.*

Clairaudience: *If you are able to hear angels or spirit guides, you are experiencing clairaudience.*

Clairkinesis: *Clairkinetics have the ability to feel the presence of angels or spirit guides. A physical sensation alerts them to the presence of an otherworldly presence.*

Clairvoyance: *A person with this type of ability*

can "see" things not apparent to others, like receiving a vision of events or a visual impression about a person.

No mind state

To be of no mind state is to be completely at one with the universe. This is not the same as when athletes say they are in the 'zone'. Being in the zone is having total focus on one thing while being of no mind state is having no focus on anything, it is the state of simply being. I am not a religious person in the church sense nor am I affiliated with any religious organization but to get across the point of no mind it is useful to use a Bible analogy.

When Jesus stated in the bible the words 'I am that I am' he was actually referring to being in a no mind state being one with everything. The native Americans say the same thing 'I am one with the trees I am one with the animals I am one with the rocks etc.' When you are of no mind state there are no reactions, no emotions, no fears, no doubts, you just are. This is what my guides have to say about no mind.

"Without self there is nothing. Emptiness I am. Without self we are one I am. Without time there is nothing emptiness I am. Without time we are one. I am."

Close your eyes. Does your mind tell you what you do not see?

Close your eyes. Do your fears and emotions dictate what you hear?

Close your eyes. Does your physical body determine the outcome your mind decrees?

I am. I am not here not there, I am. I am not afraid or fearful. I am. I am not walking, not talking. I am.

Eagle feathers.

Submitting to the I don't know is the releasing of ego the freeing of the soul it is the ultimate freedom. Only from emptiness can your body be filled.

Portious.

As a Psychic/Medium when I am with someone and I am tuned in I am of no mind state. The divine energy comes through me I speak the words, I have an awareness, but I am not attaching anything to either what is being said or the person I am with.

I am.

The reason I mention this state of 'no mind' is because it is then that we are at our most intuitive and I might add peaceful. It is the next rung of the ladder in meditation but it can also be that moment when you are completely in the now.

The advantage of being of no mind state is that you can see things with great clarity because there is not any B.S getting in the road no emotional attachment to outcomes, no judgments, no looking for agendas just what is. Why are all these things important? Part of tuning in or bringing forth the gift of insight is being able to let go of all the attachments we have.

If you want to find a state of no mind the Zazen meditation technique has been included with this lesson. Zazen is not even really meditation, because it deals with non attachment.

In Zazen, you have no goals. You can sit anywhere, but a place with few distractions would be good for beginners. Don't look at anything in particular - just emptiness, no need to focus or concentrate on anything.

SELF

This lesson is all about how to retain a sense of self and not get consumed by what you are doing. Have you ever seen someone so focused on their career that they have nothing else in their lives?

Then when they lose their job they have no idea what to do because their whole sense of self was tied to what they did. It is the same with Mothers who focus on their children and don't know who they are when their children leave home.

You need to be very aware that what you do isn't who you are. It's all about bringing spirituality into your daily life, not making it all of your life.

Its most important to understand your greatness is not one thing but many things. For example, I am a Psychic and a Medium however I am also an Artist, writer, sister, mother, spouse, mother-in-law and daughter. I read books which have nothing to do with spirituality, I have friends who do not believe in spirits and have normal everyday lives and jobs. I carve soapstone and do pencil drawing simply because I enjoy it.

Don't throw away other parts of who you are because you don't think they fit in with the new you. Being a spiritual person is about bringing the spiritual into the everyday things you do.

There is also a very big tendency for ego to creep in when you become so focused on being one thing.

So recognize you have to have more than one thing. You cannot let being an Intuitive or healer or so forth be the only thing you are. When you step into your greatness you step into infinite possibilities.

I hope I am making some sense here because I consider this to be the best piece of advice I was ever given. Don't let your passion for something turn it into an obsession. You have to have other things in your life other parts of who you are. Otherwise you run the risk of losing yourself completely!

If we succeed in making some progress, if we rise to some higher level, then we are in a position to hold out a helping hand to those who have not yet reached so high.

C.W. Leadbeater

LIFE LAYERS

Chances are you are wondering what the beep an onion has to do with being psychic. Well as I have been trying to tell you from the beginning being intuitive is about 5% of what it takes to be a good psychic.

So this lesson is all about understanding life layers. By now you might have progressed to getting a sense about people and the things around you. Or you may even be picking up words, images or feelings. Which is great but it won't do you any good unless you understand life is not one thing, it is many things all layered one on top of each other.

I might pick up that some one is having trouble in their relationship and immediately throw it out there. But chances are good I need to go deeper, stay a little longer with the feeling to 'get' what it is truly about.

So let's say I sense someone has an unhealthy relationship in which they are unhappy. First instinct may be to say 'kick his/her butt to the curb and find some one else. But if you stay with the feeling a little longer, you might start to sense another layer.

You get a sense of her/his family of origin. Maybe this is a pattern coming from unresolved childhood issues. Maybe the next relationship is doomed to end the same way. Then you might try to go a little deeper and may sense abuse or other emotional issues.

So here's the reason layers are important. If you go with the first layer you are probably putting a band aid on the problem nothing more. If you peel off the life layers eventually you will see the 'real' issues and be able to help this person grow into their greatness.

Its a fallacy that Psychics are meant to spew out information as they get it. Not that some don't but there is a lot more to operating in highest good than throwing words at people without thought or reason.

If you are to become an Intuitive you should seek be an Empath as well. That is, you must be able to walk in the other person's shoes and know what the world feels like to them.

Remember what you see on the surface rarely reflects what lies underneath. Life is not one dimensional - it is layer upon layer of moments and history. And to be an Intuitive you have to look for the layers rather than simply reflect what you see on the surface.

Its not a bad life skill to have whoever you are and whatever you do. Start practicing today with those who surround you and see if you can sit with people and get a sense of the deeper meanings behind what is going on for them.

We are all born psychic, but forget as we get older and start to use the left side of our brain.

~ John Holland ~

INTENT

Intent, what's your reason for doing what you are doing. And what's it got to do with intuitive ability?

Well if your intent is to boost your ego the information you get will probably be coming from your ego mind. If your intent is to make lots of money and the person you are reading is a means to an end, then you probably will get limited information because you are focused on your own gratification not the needs of the person in front of you.

Its not rocket science. People open up more when faced with someone genuinely interested in their wellbeing. People close down when they sense they are being used.

Intent is important for you too. It determines what you bring to you. For most intuitive workers (I hope so anyway) their intent is aligned with being of service, operating in the highest good of all humanity.

The more aligned you are with compassion, kindness, truth, the more open you will become and the more information will come to you.

Intent is when words, thoughts and action align. It is not saying one thing and doing another. It is walking your talk.

This lesson is important because having a solid, I won't say moral but ethical foundation, will ensure you in turn will be respected by those who come to you and those you work with.

I know these probably aren't the things you have been reading about in all the 'How to be a Psychic in 30 days'. Anyone can be a Psychic but not everyone can bring the greatness out in another human being, not everyone can walk their talk, not everyone will know what it feels like to unconditionally touch another soul.

Intent is the reason behind what you are doing. Am I doing it for you, am I doing it for me or am I doing for the highest good of both of us?

Intent is a very important word when applied to intuitive practices but it is also important for every aspect of our lives.

Most people assume intent aligns with actions but this isn't always the case. I can be pissed off at you and still smile and say "I think you are wonderful". A psychic can give you a bucket load of information but if their intent is simply to impress and stroke their own ego most of it will be useless to you.

When one comes back to bring through messages, many times they are of a regretful nature. They wished they knew how they should have treated people when they were alive. They wished they had loved themselves more. Most messages are indeed about love.

~James Van Praagh ~

Let's be honest, a lot of the times we do 'nice' things but expect a pay off. How many people get angry when they go out of their way for someone and don't even get a quick thank you? If you can do a good deed without the need for anyone to know about it, then you are coming from an intent of unconditional giving. As a psychic, I ask all who come to me to speak to you to come in your highest good. I ask for the wisdom to remain humble and the courage to let go of ego.

But I am human like anyone else. Yes this may come as a surprise but psychics have ego's too. There is the odd time when my partner doesn't shower me in accolades after I have done a 'nice' thing and I get all huffy which is a pretty good sign your first act wasn't unconditional.

But I am getting sidetracked. It is important to acknowledge when you have a vested interest, whether it be in getting pats on the back, or ego strokes or fame and fortune. Why? Because it gives you an indication of your intent. As a person whose purpose is to be of service to others, you should be able to give what needs to be given then let it go and walk away without a backwards glance.

My intent is always to operate in highest good and to receive the message, pass it on and let the Universe take it from there. My intent with my partner is create a happy peaceful life so whatever I do or say aligns with this intent. My intent with my children was to allow them to grow into independent confident people. So again my actions and words aligned with this intent.

So here's the deal. If you work with people and your intent is to bring them into their greatness then doing 'party tricks' or 'having a need for them to see how great you are, isn't really aligning your words and actions with that intent.

WHOSE VOICE

So you have been practicing being a good listener and about now you might be asking "how do I tell if I am talking to myself (ego) or its the Angels etc.?" That's a very good question. How do you tell if you are making it up in your head or if it is coming from an outside source? Really this comes in the form of a knowing.... you just know. Its like the gut feeling parents get when their child is in trouble or the feeling of something not being right people get when they are in dangerous situations. Its a knowing.

Having said that here are a few tips:

Ego is more likely to tell you what you want to hear than what you need to hear.

Ego will have an agenda. Angels don't.

Spirit doesn't have a day planner so exact dates are more likely to be ego.

Guides don't tend to go on and on and on but ego does.

And no Higher power will tell you to do anything which is not in the highest good of everyone involved. If you hear "run your annoying neighbour over" its probably your own voice.

It takes time and patience to learn to distinguish between ego mind and no mind. Automatic Writing is an excellent way to begin the process.

Grab a candle, a pen and a journal.

Light the candle and repeat after me:

"may all who come, come in divine light, unconditional love and for the highest good"

Then ask your Guides, Angels or Higher Power to communicate with you through the writing.

Pick the pen up and write. Don't question what you write. It doesn't matter if it doesn't make sense, you are letting the words flow on their own. You are becoming a receiver not the sender.

It takes time but allowing your thoughts to flow onto the page will help you in a couple of ways.

Firstly, you will get a sense of what may be playing on your mind and what you may not be noticing. Secondly, eventually you will connect to your soul voice on a deeper level and more meaningful words will appear.

It is good to question where stuff is coming from. I mean you wouldn't take on face value everything everyone told you in real life, would you? Sometimes psychic garbage can creep in, particularly if our intent is not aligned with the divine.

It is no good sitting down and demanding Guides give you the lotto numbers or how to win your boyfriend back. That's ego not humility.

So today's lesson is simply to listen but at the same time to try and get a feel for where the words may be coming from. Everything requires practice and patience. There aren't any shortcuts if you want to be authentic and real about being an intuitive.

CONNECT TO YOUR GUIDES

How do I connect with my guides? It may be easier than you think....

Firstly, you have to have a strong belief there is something bigger than you out there. You have to have the faith required to step where there are no steps.... but most of all you have to have patience and you have to let go of expectations. There is no right or wrong way or set time frame.

My suggestion would be to light a candle, find a quiet room and bring to your mind all those unanswered questions you have and then let them sit there.

You may like to practice automatic writing which is simply picking up a pen and writing down whatever comes into your head whether it makes sense to you or not. Guides often use this method of communication.

You might like to simply lie down with your eyes closed and picture going into a room with 2 chairs sitting on one and waiting for your guide to come sit on the other.

Whether you know it or not your guides and Angels are in constant communication with you. Those little signs that tell you maybe this would be a good idea or maybe this would not be a good idea. Or the words come into your head and you stand there thinking where did that come from?

My best piece of advice is to let go of any New Age goobly goop which says it has to be done a certain way, advice you may have read or heard. Let go of any New Age concept of what your guides should look like, talk like or should be like.

There are no rules here....

I always ask my Guides Angels Spirit, even Higher Power to come to me in unconditional love divine light and highest good.

In time you will become aware of what is your ego mind and what is not. There is a very distinct different between the two.

For example, my Guides do not tell me to do anything.... I always have the choice theirs is a guiding voice.

I do not get time frames. Spirit operates far differently than us, time is not a constraint for them.

When you hear the voice of your soul it will come from a place far removed from your head.

Again each person travels a different road so let go of expectations. When it is the right time for you to hear your guides you will hear them.

A GOOD LISTENER

Intuition isn't the gift of a few but the blessing of many. We all have it except some of us listen to it more than others.

So this lesson is all about the art of listening. This may seem silly but the first thing you have to become aware of is how much noise there is in your environment. If you can't hear yourself think with all the racket going on, chances are you aren't going to hear Creator either.

This doesn't mean you have to go find a cave, donate your children to charity or lock your partner out of the bedroom. It just means you have to find time which is yours, that is quiet, peaceful and requires you to do nothing more than be in the moment. Perhaps the best time is early morning before the noise starts or late at night when it dies down.

Basically you are finding time to have a one on one with Creator whoever and whatever you deem this to be.

Creator happens to be a very good listener so don't be surprised if he/she lets you do all the talking for a while. You need to ask for help to hear the words, and also the courage to hear them. Because often what we want to hear isn't what we need to hear. Most people I read for already know their answers - they simply don't want to acknowledge it.

It makes sense doesn't it that you would need to become a better listener in order to hear the words Guides, Angels, Creator, Spirit are trying to give you. When you begin to stop and listen, a funny thing happens. The people around you start to talk to you more.

When you take a moment for quiet chats with your partner you create intimacy. When you take a moment for quiet talks with your children, you create trust. When you take a moment to talk to your friends, you create bonds which last a lifetime. When you take a moment to talk to Creator you learn how to create what you want in your life. You also begin to hear things which before may have been whispers in the wind.

I know you want to get to the part where people jump in and out of bodies like you saw on the Medium last week but I hate to burst your bubble that's fantasy. A true Empath/Intuitive learns their craft step by step like a carpenter carving a piece of wood.

You have to become a good listener you have to take some time to connect to spirit. You cannot hear if you are always the one doing the talking. You cannot hear if the outside noise is too loud and busy or if the noise inside your head drowns out your heart voice.

Take the time to practice being a good listener. Take ten minutes a day to simply be without distraction. That's your lesson for now.

Empath: A person who can psychically tune in to the emotional experience of a person, place or animal.

CLEANSING

So you have been spending the week hugging trees and grounding yourself. Your thoughts don't keep you awake as much at night, you are calmer and more peaceful. You have managed to ground yourself. So what now?

I know you want to get to the good bits, the spooky I see dead people bits. But there are still a lot littler things to learn because what you are doing is building a strong foundation upon which you can create the life you want.

So this lesson is all about cleansing.

This again is a personal thing, so you are going to have to try a few ways before you figure out what is going to work for you.

But let's start with the why first. Energy clings, it attaches itself; this is why when you have someone sit down beside you and moan and groan about how awful their life is and how hard done by they are, you end up walking away feeling crappy and not knowing why. There are a lot of toxic people in the world and they are going to enter your life at some stage. You don't get stains on your sweater and continue to wear it without washing it neither should you wear an aura which has been stained with other people's energy.

You will notice Reiki practitioners washing their hands after each sweep across your body. Why because they are cleaning their hands of dirty energy so to speak.

So what can you do? Simple things like wash your hands, have a sea salt or lemon grass bath. I always shower after being on the presence of people whose own energy is heavy. A nice dip in the ocean is also an excellent cleanser. You don't have to do a whole heap of chanting and mix up a potion; that's the stuff of fairy tales.

Water has always been the best natural cleanser. But again do some research, try a few different things and if they work for you, then that's all that matters. But don't get caught up in a whole heap of spiritual goobly goop. Simple is always better.

You really don't want to become a bank for everyone's energy. Regardless of whether you go on to do Intuitive work, cleansing should be a way of life for everyone. When you have other people's energy attached to you it becomes difficult to sort out what's your stuff and what isn't. And when you are a psychic, the last thing you want is to become a sponge soaking up everyone else's emotions. This also goes for anyone who works in a caring profession, old age homes, counselling, youth work, nursing, teaching and even hairdressers whose chest sits right over the energy field of people's head.

So the exercise you have today is to try and find some way which works for you in terms of cleansing. If you haven't started a journal now would also be a good time to do this as well. Record your experiences around toxic people, how you felt after they left and what if anything helped cleanse your energy.

Native Americans use smudging to clean the Aura. It is the burning of certain herbs to create a cleansing smoke bath, which is used to purify people, ceremonial and ritual space, and ceremonial tools and objects.

HUMILITY

Let go of expectations and forget about making any assumptions. These are the things which will lead you to ego mind and throw objectivity out the window. The greatest threat to any intuitive is their ego mind. That's where we forget this isn't about us and it isn't coming from us. Or in other words we go from being the messenger to the one writing the message.

This lesson involves humility. Its all about service to the highest good of others and ourselves. If it is about anything else, its nothing more than an impressive party trick. With humility comes a foundation of ethical practice. You are messing with people's lives so you better have a very good moral and ethical base to stand on. Again this isn't a game and you can do a lot of damage with the wrong word said in the wrong way.

Bottom line is "if you want to teach practice what you preach". Be honest, show integrity, be humble, show humility, be to others the kind of person you would want to be reading you.

I could give you the standard "how to become a psychic" hype but we have enough frauds, fakes and people walking around with God complexes...we don't need any more.

Be humble for egos are easy things to get.

Remember to live a life which honours and respects the people around you and yourself.

You are not God so don't play God.

So this lessons exercise:

Ask yourself "why do you want to become a Psychic/Medium/Healer/whatever"

If it is simply to impress people, or because you think it will give you some sort of power over people or you think it is a nice game to amuse yourself and fill in time, then maybe you need to reconsider the next step you take.

This might surprise you but the tool you will need the most if you want to be intuitive is the ability to stay humble. The most unwanted weed in the Psychic's garden is ego. Why? Because then you start forgetting you are the instrument through which messages come.

People in general will bring into conversations subconsciously their own agenda's, opinions and beliefs. This is just part of what makes us human. No one has total objectivity when they are operating from ego mind. It's not a bad thing unless you are a psychic, because then it means you are coming from what you want someone to hear not from what the Creator (whoever you deem that to be) wants them to hear.

As a Psychic, I am purely a messenger. I deliver words, not expectations or advice on what I think you should do. I deliver words. I hand them over without any attachments and then you give them the power to create in your life. If I start thinking I am the God or Guru, then I will start adding my own little side comments in Creator's letter to you. This will result in the message not being as it was originally intended as the meaning will be lost.

Being humble is not a bad thing, whether you are a Psychic or not. The ability to walk through this life with grace and humility is one we should all aspire to.

Humility does not mean thinking less of yourself than of other people, nor does it mean having a low opinion of your own gifts. It means freedom from thinking about yourself at all.

~William Temple~

GROUNDING

To touch the earth, you must feel the ground beneath your feet.

People are like electrical wires being charged by the energy in the environment and as any good electrician will tell you, if you overload a system with too much energy, it will eventually explode. That is why there is a wire specifically used to ground electrical units. And we, as humans, are no different. We need to find a way of grounding ourselves so excess energy can be released.

Here is a list of things which indicate you are ungrounded

Mind racing with a million thoughts

Panic attacks

Indecision

The need to hurry

Increased nervousness.

Extremes in emotions

What you need to know is that grounding isn't as complicated as people make it out to be. And what works for one person may not work for another.

The first step is figuring out what works for you because not everything will. Maybe sitting under a tree will do it for you or riding a bike or gardening. Maybe a good book helps or watching a movie? For some people exercise works or a long bath with a dash of sea salt or lemon grass.

Honestly it doesn't have to be some new age way out there remedy. It is whatever brings a state of peace to you. Personally I used to go down to the beach and fish, never caught anything but it took me out of my head and into my heart.

So try out some tools find what works for you and try and become aware of what triggers you to become ungrounded so you can implement some strategies to stop it happening as often.

Becoming grounded helps you in many ways. It stops the constant flood of thoughts, it allows you the calm to be more aware of what is happening around you and when you are grounded you are more in tune with your divine source and earth Mother.

Alternatively, you can find a reputable qualified Reiki Master and ask them to ground you, which they should automatically do in any Reiki session anyway.

You can't tune into anything if your mind is like a house with every appliance turned on. You have to turn off the noise, emotions and thought processes.

This is such an important part of being intuitive you should practice it everyday. And its the reason I am not going to add anymore today.

Your homework: Go hug a tree or at least sit underneath one and lean against it. Read a book, stare at the clouds, watch life go by, and allow your body to become one with the earth.

MEDITATION

Meditation is the way most Psychics and Mediums connect with their Guides, Angels or Higher Power.

If you find the process too frustrating find a group to meditate with or see if there is anyone who runs guided meditations. There are lots of groups who meet every month to simply meditate for world peace.

Keep in mind you may not connect with anybody during your meditations but do not let that put you off. Simply taking a moment to de-stress to find balance to bring calm into your life will make your vision clearer and give you greater insight into your life situations. You will become more in 'tune' with your surroundings and the people around you.

Here I will share what my guides told me about the process of meditation and letting go of thoughts. I was told to close my eyes and visualize sitting in the middle of a big Oak tree with those massive branches reaching to the heavens and the strong thick roots reaching down into the earth. Then after I could feel myself in the Oak tree these words came to me.

'To touch the stars you must feel the Earth'

The Owl sits and allows itself to be still

Thoughts are allowed to come and go without attachment

Only when our minds are quiet

Can we see that which is before us

Allow all thoughts to come and go do not hold onto them

As they will become attached to your subconscious ego

Breathe in from the stars, Release to the Earth

Let go, breath,e feel the thoughts come and go

Allow the quiet to settle around you

It will take time

Eagle Feathers

In the beginning man survived by his senses to hunt, to gather, to mate, to survive

As these roles in man's life became obsolete so did his reliance on his senses

Close your eyes and you must see with the rest of

your body

Hear the world move. Smell the world move. Feel the world move

The blind man sees that which you cannot

You must learn to see with your eyes closed

Sit close your eyes do not imagine the world around you for this is an illusion of mind

See the world around you using the senses that you have neglected

Eagle Feathers

Eagle Feathers makes a very good point about seeing with your eyes closed. You will find most blind people have heightened senses and a greater level of intuitiveness than people who can see. Sitting with your eyes closed and really trying to listen to the world with your other senses decreases your reliance on sight (the visual).

Some people after sitting for a while doing this actually find themselves unaware of time and where they are some even enter a meditative state. But the real beauty of heightened senses is the world becomes a different place and you no longer rush unaware of that which surrounds you. I personally would start with this exercise of closing your eyes then move on to the traditional Meditation. For a lot of people meditation is defined as a state of not having any thoughts but this is not the case.

When I first started meditating I was so worried about not thinking any thoughts that my mind just filled with thoughts about not having thoughts!!!! The trick is to let the thoughts come and go without being attached to them. Think of any thoughts that enter as little white clouds that you watch drift away. Eventually with practice you will find fewer thoughts entering and your mind will wander less.... keep in mind people who get to a stage of pure non attachment in meditation usually practice every day.

There are a lot of misconceptions in regards to meditation, the main one being it is a new age practice where people go into another dimension. Meditation can be, as Adam Sandlar learnt in the movie Happy Gilmour, simply a case of teaching yourself to go off to your happy place. Doing something calming and relaxing can be a form of meditation; getting lost in a good book, painting, cooking or putting on some soft music, closing your eyes, and drifting to the sounds.

For some praying can be a form of meditation going within to seek guidance from a higher power. Chanting for other religions becomes a tool for meditation. It is what works for you that matters what takes you to that place of peace where all is well in your world.

There are no rules but I will give a couple of guidelines that may be helpful.

Concentrating on breathing can help focus you inward.

Being aware of each breath as it enters and leaves your body

Don't get preoccupied with emptying your head of thoughts the more you focus on your thoughts the more will come just let them come and go like watching the clouds above you.

Try to ground before you start or use the meditation itself as a grounding agent.

Try to take a comfortable posture

Don't force it. If it doesn't seem to be working try something different.

Exercise: This is the loving kindness meditation. Take a comfortable position, focus on your chest and breath in and out from that area. You may close your eyes or choose to leave them open. Breath in and out several times each time letting go of any negative feelings you have towards yourself. Then say to yourself out loud or just in your head

May I be safe and protected May I be free of suffering

May I be healthy and strong

May I be able to live in this world happily, peacefully

and with joy

Next think about someone who makes you feel really good about yourself repeat the affirmations for them

May you be safe and protected

May you be free from suffering

May you be healthy and strong

May you be able to live in this world happily, peacefully and with joy

Then move on to someone you have difficulty with who you do not feel loving kindness for and say

To the best of my ability I wish you to be safe and protected

To the best of my ability I wish you free from suffering

To the best of my ability I wish you health and strength

To the best of my ability I wish you peace, happiness and joy

Lastly we want to send loving kindness all beings May *all beings be safe, happy and live with joy.* Repeat this line several times You can shorten this meditation to

May I be safe from harm

May I be happy as I am

May I be peaceful no matter what is happening

May I be healthy and strong

May my world be filled with joy happiness and peace

Then end with *may all living beings everywhere be safe, happy, healthy and free from suffering.*

PSYCHIC GOSSIP

This is when information is picked up one way or the other and shared without thought or consideration.

I pick up 'stuff' all the time about people but it is not my place to go up to these people and say this is what I see, hear or get from you. That is Psychic Gossip it is unethical and dangerous and shows a lack of mentoring on the part of the intuitive involved.

Some people are not ready to hear things, some people have to find it out for themselves, it is a life lesson and yep sometimes it is none of my business. Just because I have an intuitive gift doesn't give me the right to poke my Psychic antenna into someone else's life.

Sometimes what we get as Psychics fits into a bigger picture and we may only be getting a small piece of the puzzle. It is not our job to enlighten everyone and share everything we pick up to perfect strangers on the street. This is often the case though with people who have awakened to their intuitive gift and have not been mentored in how to use it in a way which honours all involved. The first impulse is

Creator would not give me this gift if he/she didn't want me to share it with everyone. "Hey you, person I have never meant before, did you know your husband is having an affair? Oops sorry I didn't mean to, break up a home, shatter a family and send your children into therapy."

Intuitiveness is a gift but it is also a tool that is used to create and yet has the capacity to hurt as well. Psychic Gossip the sharing of information which has been picked up by eavesdropping in someone's energy is a very dangerous practice. So please, if you are developing your intuitive gifts, recognize the ethical responsibilities which come with it. Be aware that people's lives are not personal playgrounds and every word is a ripple that creates consequences which may be felt long after.

Know that you are human and being intuitive does not rid you of ego, in fact it highlights it. It is very easy to get caught up in wanting the light to shine on you rather than through you. Find a mentor build a foundation of ethical practices and know it is a gift that needs to be unwrapped slowly with great care and awareness.

Most people think psychics don't read anyone under 18 for legal reasons and that's partly true.

And I can only speak for myself when I say there are

many other reasons why it isn't a good idea.

Firstly, children and teenagers are still forming their identity, finding out who they are in the world and where they belong. Part of this process is making mistakes and learning from them. What kids don't need is some psychic sticking their nose into what is part of the growing up process.

Kids need to experiment, explore and work out who they are on their own. They don't need to know the future they need to learn how to make good choices which will create the future they want.

Don't take your kids to a psychic don't put the weight of the future on their shoulders - they don't need that. Allow them to find out for themselves how they fit into this world. We all went through it and it is selfish to deny the journey to your children.

EMPATHY

If you want to be intuitive start by developing empathy. Empathy being the ability to feel, know and understand what it is like to be in someone else's shoes.

If I do not possess empathy, I might as well give up my day job of being a psychic, because I am not going to truly feel you, even with the most wonderful psychic abilities.

The thing about this skill is it requires you to be in the moment. You cannot have empathy for someone when they are baring their soul to you and you are in the future planning the grocery list.

You have to be totally unconditionally there.

Intuitive people feel.... I repeat they feel...how can you tell a person who has this skill? They listen rather than speak.... they listen rather than attempt to fix.... they can stop their minds long enough to listen to their hearts.

It is all well and good to want to be the next

Sylvia Browne but you would touch more lives in a far more meaningful way and even change more lives by simply tuning in to the people around you.

Developing skills such as empathy tunes you into life. It requires you to become aware of subtle things such as body language, the things not spoken.

I am not just tuning into the energy when I am reading someone, I am tuning into their life, their worries, their fears, doubts and insecurities.

If I did not have the ability the skill of empathy, I might miss the subtle changes needed to nudge people into their greatness. I might give the broad outline of jobs, careers, travel, family....and miss the moment where a simple "I know that has to be tough for you" might have made all the difference.

FACE TO FACE READINGS

First of all, relax. Your guides, the Angels, Creator have it all under control. Your job is to put the person sitting opposite you at ease. They are probably as nervous as you are!

Start with some house keeping. Ask if they have any questions about what you do and be forthcoming and honest with your replies.

Put them at ease by giving a brief outline of how things will progress, reassure them you aren't going to tell them they have only months to live or are going to drive their car over a cliff. If you do not do predictions state so up front, if you do not do medical, financial or legal questions state so up front.

You want to speak clearly and ask often if they understand what you are saying.

Make it clear at the start that you are the psychic and that being the case, its your job to tune into them, not their job to give you their full resume. If you don't want to be accused of cold reading, then make sure you stop your sitter from talking non stop through out the reading. Getting confirmation, you are on the right track is entirely differently than pushing a sitter into revealing information about themselves.

Don't take back what you have said. If the sitter doesn't gel with the words, then they don't gel.

Nothing is worst than a psychic who back tracks and tries to rearrange the message so it makes them look better. Just remember, sometimes the sitter isn't going to acknowledge things they don't want to acknowledge. Sometimes the sitter isn't going to remember something happened or someone they knew. Best to say okay, we don't seem to be on the right track, so let's move on.

Always remember to take your time.... don't panic if the sitter gets push. Simply take a breath refocus and you can even reassure the sitter by saying something like "information sometimes takes a little longer to come through but that's okay if we go 10 minutes over you won't be charged extra". Every one likes to think they are getting something for nothing so offering some extra time usually gets people to calm down. And worst case scenario, nothing comes then offer to refund the money and again be honest and say "I am not getting any info and don't want to go in circles and waste your time". Honesty is always the best policy.

By creating a conversation at the beginning of the reading, and putting the sitter at ease, you are going to have a much more pleasurable experience. The same goes for making sure you have at least 1/2 an hr before the reading to sit and breathe and relax. All preparation work should be done well in advance. If you have to set up cards, tables, chairs or what ever tools you use then do so as early on as you can.

I find people relate to me better when I am just being me, when I am making them feel comfortable being in my presence, when I am being open and honest about who I am and what I do because the walls people put up will come down a lot easier if they can trust and believe in you.

This applies to both Mediumship and Psychic Work.

Mediumship Basics

People who have lost someone they love are usually very emotional, vulnerable and have a great need to have understanding.

So my first words of advice would be to make sure people have had time to grieve, because the steps in the grieving process should never be skipped over in favour of a session with a Medium. People need to walk through anger, denial, sadness and pushing these feelings aside will only create more pain in their lives. So maybe before you even start out as a Medium, you should familiarize yourself with the grieving process so you can recognize in the people who come to you where they are at and how you should approach the session. Or whether they should have a session at all.

People in spirit as a general rule do not carry pagers so don't say you can bring Uncle Bob in when in fact you can only work with those in spirit who chose to be there with you.

Spirit as a general rule, will give the information which the sitter will relate to most. I remember having a man is spirit telling me to say "its okay I won't shoot Bambi" this made no sense to me at all and I hesitated to relay the message. But it turns out the sitter had said that to her grandfather many times as a child before he went out hunting.

Which brings me to my next point. It may not make sense to you but the reality is the message isn't for you! So share the information as it comes in rather then censor it because it sounds rather odd.

As with psychic readings, ask the sitter to sit quietly and only speak when you need clarity that you are on the right track. Nothing bugs me more than when a Medium says I see a man behind you and the sitter goes that must be my grandfather and then the Medium goes "oh yes it is" when in fact up until that point all they were sensing was a male presence. Its dishonest, disrespectful and reflects badly on those of us who are genuine in what we do. I have no hesitation shutting a sitter down and asking they refrain from saying anything until I have gotten more information. I don't need to prove anything to anyone.

That's not my job. My job is to make sure the sitter gets the message from the person in spirit who is there and who usually, I might add has a reason to be there.

Be careful to take things slowly when you are first starting out. There was one case of a Medium who gave a message to a woman in which the woman's Aunty suggested the woman's child be taken off medication and given something else. In this true case the woman's child died. I have said it before and I will say again words have great power so while you should deliver them uncensored you should also be double checking where they are coming from and whether it is in the sitters highest good to hear them. I am going to get a lot of people arguing with me on this but I stand by it.

Experience has shown that sometimes Mediums misinterpret what is coming to them so a little double checking isn't a bad thing. And there are ways and means of relaying information. If there is a health concern a better approach may be simply to say your Uncle is concerned about your health and suggests you go to the Doctor or your Aunty is concerned about this legal contract you are entering into and suggests you go get it checked by a lawyer.

Bottom line is you are not a Doctor nor are you a Lawyer or a broker or marriage counsellor or psychologist. Its what I spoke to earlier about recognizing what's your job and what isn't. By all means if Uncle Bob is saying the person in front of you needs to dump their husband then suggest they see a counsellor or build their relationship skills.

If Aunty Jane is saying the person in front of you is going to lose all their money, then go with suggesting they need to reassess their finances and seek professional help to manage them. But telling them they are going to go broke serves no higher purpose at all.

Most of all remember to treat spirit with

respect and dignity, as you would any living being.

DIFFERENT READINGS

Don't limit yourself to one type of reading - experiment a little. As my friend said when asked if she could read hands "I can read hands, toes, ears anything you want.... within reason."

If you are intuitive you should be able to read any body part because what you are doing is reading the energy which surrounds a person.

Reading feet by massage: Invite a group of friends around and give them foot massages and see what you can pick up. There is a certain way my hands react when I do this and its instinctive and to hard to explain but I guarantee whether or not you get any information will be of little concern because most people love a good foot massage and it's a great gift to give those you care about!

Reading energy from objects: Again invite a group of friends over, put a basket at the front door where they can throw their jewellery in and not have you see it. Then try and read the energy by enclosing each piece in your hand. I find it better to do this as then those in the room do not know who's earring etc. you have either. And they will have fun trying to figure out who you are talking about.

Keep it simple. For example, I sense this person is very organized and tidy or make it a bit of fun by saying I sense this person will find hidden treasure and maybe the cat buried under the clothes in their bedroom. Short sentences are better than long drawn out ones.

Reading names: This is not really something you can teach because it is mainly intuitive but here are some tips

Don't try and SEE anything let the name tell you

Look at the way it sits on the page does it seem big or small does it seem to lean one way or the other?

Does the name appear to fade in or come forward?

Let the words and images come to you then interpret the symbolism not by what some book says but by what that object means to you. If I see flowers I see abundance

Reading through your body: I feel people through my body. If my shoulders get heavy, it suggests the person is carrying a weight or burden. If I am pulled backwards it means a connection to the past. If my legs, feel heavy it means they may be stuck in a rut. If my vision gets blurry maybe they lack clarity. You just have to learn to listen to what your body is telling you; it will come with experience and awareness. When you are sitting next to someone on the bus or at a movie theatre or where ever try becoming aware of how their energy is making your body feel.

Try different tools: I have a little old lady friend who reads tea leaves and ordinary playing cards. Another friend of mine reads through using flowers. You don't have to make these things part of your practice but it pays to shake the cobwebs out every now and then by trying new things!

Psychic Parties: These don't have to be the stereotype grab a person and drag them into a dark room type of thing. You can and should make them fun and interesting, not everything has to be all seriousness. Try some of the different things we have mentioned. I personally use Kinder eggs and get people to see how intuitive they are by guessing what's inside them. Play games, get people involved in what's happening, partner them up ask them to use telepathy to tell the other person what colour Smarties they are holding in their hand. Give away prizes such as a free reading or pick up some Halloween Gifts like spooky cups and such like. The possibilities are endless.

I never limit myself by saying this is the way I should be doing this (the exception being the ethical and moral guidelines I always follow). I let my guides do what they do best.... guide me. Every person you read and every situation will be different.

DREAM INTERPRETATION

Dreams are the rivers of the subconscious flowing into our thoughts, bringing all those things we have tried to hide in the deep recesses of our mind. Dreams are many things. They are the way Angels, Guides and loved ones passed can make contact with us without fear of frightening us with their presence.

Symbolism is the traditional way of interpreting dreams but it is important to note different people will attach different meaning to certain objects. What the ocean means to me might not be what it means to you. Dream weaving is unravelling dreams so their meaning can be revealed to us and it is this task we take on now.

The first thing to do is break down the dream into parts. Start by looking for symbols example a house, car, water Don't limit yourself to the obvious look for numbers, letters or colors also. Figure out what you are doing in the dream what actions reactions, emotions, are there. Look at what you have written does anything evoke an emotional response?

Try to figure out why.

What events took place in the dream and what would be your relationship to those happenings in real life? Can you link the meaning of a symbol with what might be happening in your life something you are afraid of, trying to avoid, want to have happen in the future? Once you have done all of the above, sit back and try to look at the dream as a jigsaw puzzle waiting to be solved. Things to keep in mind All symbols are open to interpretation don't rely on the meanings to heavily try to thinking what does this symbolize to me?

Not every dream needs to be interpreted. A lot of dreams are our minds having a spring cleaning or they may simply reflect something we watched on the television or read in the media that affected us more profoundly than we first thought. Keep writing in your dream journal that way you will know if there are reoccurring themes. Keep it by your bed so you can write in it upon waking.

Perhaps the most common thing dreamt about is a house. Houses are thought of as our self. What part of the house you dream about, also has it's own separate meaning. Perhaps it is better to sit down and describe in detail the house in your dreams and relate this information back to how you might be feeling about yourself. Is the house falling down- Are you struggling to define who you are? Are you on the outside of the House? Are you being what others want you to be? Are you trapped in the House? Do you hate parts of yourself? You may even want to see what is in the house and relate that back to how you feel about yourself. Are there any windows? Do you feel lack of opportunity in your life?

Vehicles, cars etc. are also a major symbol because they are said to represent your journey. When you dream about a car, look for things like where it is headed, who is driving, or what type of car it is. For example, if you are in the passenger seat and some one else is driving then maybe at some level you feel others are in control of the direction your life is taking. If you are not in the car, ask yourself what may be keeping you from moving in the direction of your dreams?

Again look for other symbols that may indicate obstacles in your way. Is the car old and rusty? Maybe its time to try new ideas and a different approach to your life journey? As you can see, once you have a basic idea of what the symbols are in your dream and a good description of them, you will be able to apply your own interpretations.

Water is another common symbol and as with the car/house analogy you need to think about all aspects of its appearance. Water is said to represent our emotions and is also a symbol for the unconscious. But its interpretation is very subjective because a large body of water may be peaceful to you but be a symbol of being out of my depth to me. So when you start your dream journal, and you come across a symbol like an ocean or lake write down what emotional response it evokes and use this as your interpretation guideline.

There are certain events that are common in dreams. Falling is often associated with fear of losing control or may reflect a sense of failure, drowning the inability to handle situations in your life or loss of emotional control and being chased usually symbolizes your fear of something or chasing something and trying to get rid of something from your life. A bridge is usually transition or transformation.

A baby/birth a new beginning or new ideas.

Sample Dream Interpretation:

I looked out the window at my parent's house, and saw a dark horse. It looked like it was stiff and decaying, I say to myself "it's petrified", I was thinking like petrified wood or something.

Then I see the horse alive and bucking frantically, children are being put on top of it to ride and the horse is going mad. The adults don't seem to be afraid to keep putting the kids on this horse. I am watching feeling very scared for both the horse and the kids on it.

Meaning of significant symbols, themes and messages:

Horse: As a Totem animal, horse's medicine is speed, endurance, power and freedom of spirit. Dark horses are meant to symbolize the unknown, the mystical. If the horse is bucking, then it is tied to things being out of control.

Decay: Can be associated with a situation which is worsening or it may indicate the old has to die for the new to be reborn.

Children: Are representative of our inner child and to standing, watching them, would mean you are not seeing something, either in yourself such as potential, or there is knowledge yet to be discovered.

Parents: Are our shelter, our protectors they represent both love and power.

Fear: Is the same in dreams as in real life, it is reminders of our anxieties and worries.

Looking out of a Window: Is related to awareness, vision and intuitiveness. It may indicate reflection, soul searching or looking deeper inside of yourself.

Overall Interpretation:

This dream to me symbolizes a very powerful stage in your life right now and perhaps changes which have shifted you out of your comfort zone. It may also indicate you are afraid of your own power and the fear you feel is that of someone being challenged to step out of the familiar into the unknown.

The fact the adults aren't afraid to put the children on the horse may mean you have people around you who believe in your potential but you are either not listening or not aware of the support you have. Sometimes we have to let go of old beliefs about who we are and what we are capable of in order to step into our full potential.

The fact you are looking out of your parent's window may indicate you feel safe in the familiar, the known, but do not trust your own ability to handle stepping into the unknown. I feel you do not trust yourself as much as you should and Horse has come to teach you take back your power over your little self. But the old may have to die before the new you can re-emerge.

Some Tips

I have been doing readings all my life in the form of advice and insight given to friends and family and the occasional stranger sitting on a bar stool or at a bus stop. But I didn't open up my heart and soul to my pathway until I was in my mid 30's. There have been certain lessons I have learned along the way which I would like to share with you now.

Lesson 1: It is not always your job to help, advise or step in. This is a big misconception people starting out have. For example, one year I volunteered at a camp for disadvantaged youth. My job was to do a meditation with them and talk about spirituality which I did, and it went very well. Then I stayed and helped out for a while. There were other speakers and I listened in on their workshops and to my surprise was slightly jealous of how they were able to engage the children. I remembered taking a walk afterwards and hearing these words from my guides "there are many spokes in the wheel which make it turn and you are but one".

I was able to recognize my ego had been in play and began to understand sometimes you have to step aside and allow someone else to do the job creator set for them. Its something which only comes with experience the inner knowing "this isn't my job". But it always pays to ask because when you step in when you are not meant to you may prevent the person getting the help she/he really needs.

Side Note: You are not required to read everyone who comes to you or asks to be read.

Lesson 2: Know when to stop. Again this only comes with experience. I had a woman come to me once for a reading I told her that her father was with us in spirit and was talking about her 2 teenage children and how they were walking down a destructive path and needed some guidance. Her father also spoke of being sorry for emotional abuse and various other things. The woman turned to me and said "I don't want to know about all of that I want to know when Mr. Right is coming and how will I recognize him?" I tried to tell her "if I tell you he is a plumber with a blue car you will just stalk plumbers with blue cars until one goes out with you.... doesn't make me a great psychic but may turn you into a stalker!"

So here's the thing she wasn't in a place to hear what she needed to hear. She had already decided what she wanted to hear and nothing else would do. So I stopped the reading and refunded her money. If I hadn't done this, we would have gone round and round in circles and telling her Mr. Right was coming might have lined my wallet but it wouldn't have helped her at all.

Lesson 3: You don't have to be nor should you try to be, like anyone else. When I first started I tried to be like my friend who has been a medium for 30 years. She gets things like your car is blue, you have 2 cats, and 3 children. Me - I kept getting emotions and feelings more than anything so I thought I wasn't a very good psychic. I tried doing Tarot cards because I thought they would make me look legitimate but truth is you have to follow your own pathway.

My friend has her job to do, I have mine, we do things differently but it doesn't mean I have any less psychic ability or my job is less important. Don't try and be a James Van Praag or a John Edwards, let your gifts develop naturally on their own. You will know what feels right for you and what doesn't and make sure to honour this. Be the best you that you can be.

Lesson 4: You don't have to be a psychic reader just because you can read people nor do you have to be a Medium just because you see dead people. This is another common misconception. My son is psychic and he uses his intuitive ability in his business and uses the profits from his business to give back to the community. Some people use their gifts as counsellors, teachers, elder and community care, the possibilities are endless and each just as meaningful and worthwhile.

Let go of the stereotype images, there is so much more open to you than crystal balls and tarot cards.

Lesson 5: Steps on the ladder. We never stop

learning and there is always something for us to learn. But here's the thing. I can do what I do because my body raises its vibration to match the vibration of the spirit energy which surrounds me. It is something which has been a gradual progression over time. When I finished one lesson and my guides thought I was ready for it everything went up a notch. People get into trouble, particularly with energy from those in spirit, because they open themselves up to too much energy and their body simply isn't ready or equipped to handle it.

Often this is what people mistake as 'bad' or 'negative entities', it's the overload of energy which creates the shaking, the body trembles, the feeling of overload not some spirit out to get you. Its like opening the door but forgetting to close it again. With time these feelings will subside as you get more accustomed to the different energy levels. But be careful not to play with things you do not fully understand and start off small before you start opening the door to anyone who knocks.

Lesson 6: Ego: I talked about it earlier but it is worth repeating, because I have seen so many people, some of many years' experience, develop what they call God complexes. What we receive in terms of messages come through us, not from us. We are still the ones interpreting the messages but to be an open channel one cannot have ego mind in play.

When we start developing egos and start believing we are Guru's and God's then we start projecting our own judgments and bias into the reading and we lose objectivity. That's what no mind is about - not becoming attached to the message. For example, if I start putting personal opinion into my readings, then I am coming from ego "I think your weight issues are because you are lazy" or "I would do this or that if I was you". Or I might start making judgments "I see you are a cleaner you should get another job it would make you feel better about yourself".

Objectivity implies no attachment to the sitter's emotion, to the situation, to the words being given. When I read for some one, the moment the reading ends, I forget what was said. And there is a reason for this - its because its not about me, the message was for them and them alone. Another reason we practice non attachment or no mind is because we don't want to become energy sponges which soak up everything because we would burn out very quickly.

Lesson 7: Ethics, this isn't a hard one to explain. If you wouldn't want it done to you then don't do it to someone else. Be truthful in thought and deed and if you don't get any information then be honest and say so. Every one's ethical base is going to be different depending on their belief system. For me I don't do predictions because I believe the future is created in the present and I want to empower people to find their own answers.

It may not be very profitable but money is never my motivation - highest good is. I don't do reading for anyone under 18 and I don't share information without first asking permission. Bottom line is we all need some sort of ethical base for our intuitive practice- a set of guidelines of things we will and will not do. It is up to you to build yours and again this will change as your perceptions of the world and your place in it change.

Lesson 8: Accuracy. No one I don't care who they are is always going to be 100% accurate and only those with ego issues will go around claiming otherwise. Which is why you should be very careful walking into areas such as medical issues, financial issues, legal issues and so on. You are not all knowing. Misinterpretation of messages received has been known to happen and psychics have off days too. Again you can't take back the words once they are spoken and people tend to take the words of a psychic as gospel. So choose yours wisely.

ABOUT THE AUTHOR

Robin Roberts is an Australian Psychic and Medium currently residing on Vancouver Island of the coast of British Columbia Canada. Over the last 30 yrs. she has sought to bring what she terms 'simple wisdom' into the lives of the people who come to her. She hopes through her writing to lead people to the corners of their souls so they may rediscover the people they were born to be. As a Psychic she offers a unique perspective on personal transformation and the challenges facing all of us.

Find out more at islandlifecoach.com

OTHER BOOKS BY ROBIN ROBERTS

What do I do now

How to become a master

Life Mapping

How to become a Butterfly

Love gives us wings

The little human who could

165 Life Lessons

Get out of your head

I simply am

Manufactured by Amazon.ca
Bolton, ON